Francis Bour.

Diocesan seminaries and the education of ecclesiastical students

Francis Bourne

Diocesan seminaries and the education of ecclesiastical students

ISBN/EAN: 9783741155871

Manufactured in Europe, USA, Canada, Australia, Japa

Cover: Foto ©Lupo / pixelio.de

Manufactured and distributed by brebook publishing software
(www.brebook.com)

Francis Bourne

Diocesan seminaries and the education of ecclesiastical students

DIOCESAN SEMINARIES

AND THE

EDUCATION OF ECCLESIASTICAL

STUDENTS.

BY

FRANCIS A. BOURNE,

RECTOR OF ST. JOHN'S DIOCESAN SEMINARY, WONERSH.

LONDON: BURNS & OATES, LIMITED.
NEW YORK, CINCINNATI, CHICAGO : BENZIGER BROTHERS.

PREFACE.

It seems necessary to explain why the following articles were communicated to the *Tablet*, and why they are now reprinted with additional matter. On March 4th an article appeared in that paper strongly advocating the union of the Southern dioceses of England in a joint central Seminary. There were grave reasons for doubting either the practicability or the advantage of such a course, while it seemed clear that more than one diocese was in a position to have its own Seminary. The Diocese of South-wark was already committed to a policy incompatible with the proposal. Until recent years its clergy had been, for the most part, educated with the Westminster students at St. Edmund's College, and at St. Thomas' Seminary, Hammersmith ; but some twenty years ago it was intimated to Southwark that it must make provision for the training of its own clergy. This was only carrying out the policy decreed by the Fourth Synod of Westminster, and earnestly enforced by the late Cardinal Archbishop. No choice was left to Southwark in the matter. It be-came necessary, therefore, to provide a Seminary for this diocese, so that there might be some institution for the education of its clergy. A considerable sum of money was collected, and after many delays a beginning was made four years ago. Southwark, therefore, acting in obedience to authority, has

4

provided sufficiently for itself, and is carrying out a long-conceived clearly defined policy, which it can hardly reverse, or exchange for a completely new departure. It seemed a necessity, then, to explain in the *Tablet* that the proposed scheme was an impossible one for at least one diocese, and that it seemed undesirable in other respects. I was naturally lead to show that a Seminary is possible when a diocese has attained a certain development, and to speak of its government, course of studies, and the rest.

The following articles are now published in deference to a wish which claims not only ready compliance, but almost obedience. This must be my excuse if I appear presumptuous in treating such important questions. The first two articles are reprinted exactly as they appeared in the *Tablet*. Although a few points may have lost their actuality, and there may be a want of sequence owing to the circumstances under which the articles were written, it has been thought better to leave them unchanged. The substance of the third article was written as a reply to the rejoinder of the *Tablet* (March 25th), but it was considered expedient to defer the publication; it is now given here in a more complete form. The fourth article discusses more fully some important questions raised in the first. I am assured that these articles may be of interest to those conversant with the subject, and I trust that this will be the case.

F. A. B.

St. John's Diocesan Seminary,
  Wonersh, Guildford.
Feast of St. John before the Latin Gate,
  May 6th, 1893.

CONTENTS.

ON DIOCESAN SEMINARIES AND THE EDUCATION OF ECCLESIASTICAL STUDENTS.

———

I. Some Remarks on the Proposed Establishment of a Central Seminary.

Tablet, March 11th, 1893.

The question of the education of aspirants to the Priesthood is one of so much interest, and fraught with such grave consequences to the well-being of a diocese, that we venture to ask to be allowed to make some remarks on certain aspects of the question. If it is considered that the policy of the last twenty years has been mistaken, and a policy of centralisation is being advocated, we trust that we shall not be regarded as presumptuous in setting forth some points which are at least worth consideration, lest in another twenty years we may again be found on the wrong path.

1. It is conceded in the article of last Saturday that "the separate Diocesan Seminary is the Church's ideal," but the writer proceeds as though no dioceses in the South were in a position to act up to this ideal, and to stand alone. He suggests the union of all in a central college. It will be readily admitted that the best and only method for several of the Southern dioceses is to coalesce for a time, until they can act independently ; for it would be a misfortune if a central college were to retard the legitimate development of a diocese in the direction of

an independent Seminary.* But what is to be said
of the greater dioceses, *e.g.*, Westminster and
Southwark? For more than forty years Westminster has had within its own jurisdiction a college
for the education of its clergy. Most have recognised the unavoidable necessity of parting with St.
Thomas's. Edmundians, however, rejoiced in the
hope and thought that Old Hall would now be
restored to its former position, and that the clergy
of the Archdiocese would again receive their entire
formation within its venerable and cherished walls.
Ought not this to be? Southwark is providing
amply for the eighty or ninety students required to
keep pace with its ever growing needs. It will
have accommodation in its own Seminary for more
than one hundred students, from their entrance on
Humanities at fourteen till the *completion of their
Divinity*, and will admit ecclesiastical students only.
Southwark, therefore, hardly seems to need a central
college. Can it be said that these two large and
important dioceses would be more in harmony with
the mind of the Council of Trent by making use of
a joint Seminary in another diocese than by using
their own resources?

2. The writer says truly that "the Seminary of
the Council started with Humanities." The age of
admission was *ad minimum duodecim annos.* St.

* The provision made by the Council of Trent, allowing poor
dioceses to unite in a common Seminary, evidently refers to dioceses
the *normal* state of which happens to be one of poverty. It does not
apply in the same way to the dioceses of a missionary country, which
are in a *progressive* state of development. In such, a joint Seminary
will be a temporary expedient, not a permanent arrangement.

Charles put the age at fifteen as being the most suitable age for beginning Humanities. But the article continues : " If our existing colleges are in harmony with the mind of the Council, etc." Can this hypothesis be admitted ? Our colleges, with their mingling of lay and Church students, have done an admirable work ; but for the very reason of this intermingling they are not Seminaries *ad mentem Concilii*. The Council meant separation : " In hoc collegio recipiantur . . . quorum indoles et voluntas spem afferat eos ecclesiasticis ministeriis perpetuo inservituros." Craisson, Zitelli, and others, repeat this condition at the present day as essential to the nature of a true Seminary (see for a fuller treatment Pouän, *De Seminario Clericorum*). Peremptory reasons have caused the union of the two classes in England, and it is for the Bishops alone to decide how long the need continues, but it is not *ad mentem Concilii*. Nowhere is this more clearly recognised than in our own Provincial Councils, held under Cardinal Wiseman. In the First Council of Westminster it is said : " Summopere religionis augmento profuturum putamus, si seminaria in quibus *seorsim* educarentur clerici, possent fundari." In the Third Council we find : " *Unicum* pro hoc defectu (worldliness) remedium certe est segregatio Clericorum a laicis." Worldliness is more prevalent now than it was thirty or forty years ago, or than it was at the time of the Council of Trent. If the reasons alleged by the Councils of Trent and Westminster are valid, the separation would seem to have become more urgent. It is between the ages of fourteen and twenty that character is developed and formed ; if a solid foundation of supernatural virtue is laid then, it will probably last, but it will be laid with much greater difficulty later on, save in exceptional cases We are able to speak not in theory, but with knowledge of facts and of both methods, when we say that, although there are advantages to be derived from the union of the ecclesiastical and lay students during the years from fourteen to eighteen or twenty, they are out-weighed by the disadvantages. On the other hand, we can testify that the benefits of strictly carrying out the Tridentine directions on this point are immeasurable. Students under this latter system soon find out the reality or absence of vocation : they thus take to other occupations in good time, and thereby they avoid injury to their future prospects and unnecessary expense. Those who persevere can be allowed much greater liberty and treated with a confidence and trust which are not attainable in a mixed college. Above all, they can be trained on a much higher and more solid spiritual level. These are some of the advantages, and they are not to be disregarded. Père de Foresta, the saintly founder of the Apostolic schools, speaking of the almost universal union of clerical and lay students in the *Petits Séminaires* in France, said : "Would not the decree of the Council of Trent have produced much more abundant fruits if it had been carried out in all the dioceses, and especially if the *Petits Séminaires* had preserved the exclusively ecclesiastical character which the Fathers of the Council wished to give to them?" There can be but one answer from those who have practical experience of the two systems.

3. Another point of interest is the course of studies to be pursued in a central college. Is it to be a Seminary course in preparation for parochial work, or a course of higher, quasi-University, studies? By all means let us have the latter if we are ripe for it, but it seems a mistake to attempt to unite the two. Two chief systems have been followed in different places for the intellectual formation of the clergy. The first is to make students go through a long course of study, such as that followed in the Gregorian University: this is excellent for students of more than average capacity. The other system is to have a shorter course, embracing a solid grounding in all the subjects required for parochial work, but necessarily of an elementary character. All students of the diocese go through this ordinary course, and at *the end* of it those who have special talent are sent to a college of Higher Studies, or to a University, to perfect themselves in some special subject or subjects of study. The Seminary precedes and is distinct from the University. Each has its appointed function. The Seminary undertakes the spiritual formation and elementary theological training of all students; the University is for the more perfect intellectual development of the more gifted, whose spiritual

formation has been already attended to, who are already in Holy Orders, and whose minds are somewhat matured by their previous studies and so prepared for a higher course. This is the method usually followed in France and Belgium, and, we believe, in the United States ; and it seems the more reasonable in ordinary cases. By making all students pass through an elaborate course of Philosophical and Theological study, in aiming at much little will be obtained. Anyone acquainted with an average class of Divines will admit that only a small number will profit by a very extended course, while the mental capacity of the remainder will be overburdened by a mass of undigested matter. The majority of those called to the Priesthood (or to any state of life) are of average ability, and with a simpler course they will attain the solid *scientia competens*, which they need to be good parish priests, and will do excellent work. It is not necessary that every priest should be a genius, able to be a Master or even a Licentiate of Divinity, any more than that every medical practitioner should be a consulting physician, or every lawyer a Q.C. We should be sorry to depreciate the need of learning in the clergy : that some should be of the highest possible culture and attainments is most desirable, but this is possible to very few. A Seminary course is meant for the average student. How few are considered able to profit by these advanced studies may be learned from other countries. In Belgium, for example, education is well organised, and the system here advocated is followed. The students go through the whole, or nearly the whole, of an elementary course in their Diocesan Seminaries ; then, when they are already deacons or priests, the picked men pass on to Louvain. How many do so every year ? Less than thirty, we believe, and there must be hundreds of students of Philosophy and Divinity in the various Seminaries of the country. Again, out of the sixty or more ecclesiastics who are usually at Louvain, only about thirty are studying Theology or Canon Law, while the remainder are occupied with Literature or Mathematics, etc., in order later on to profess these subjects in their own dioceses. Formerly, students who had not been through an elementary course elsewhere were allowed to follow the lectures at Louvain, but of later years this has been discouraged if not prohibited, as it was found that such students were not able to derive advantage from these higher studies. The Sulpicians, whose experience in the education of the clergy is certainly unequalled, hold strongly to the same view (*v.* Icard, *Traditions de la Compagnie de S. Sulpice*, p. 399). The Third Council of Baltimore also says, that students may proceed to a higher course "consueto studiorum absoluto cursu . . . ordinariorum studiorum curriculum emensi."* We would express an earnest

° See also *Conc. Prov. Westm. IV.* (Decr. IX. 13): "E numero alumnorum qui ingenio et studio praestant nonnulli pro arbitrio Episcopi seligi possunt, qui, *curriculo praescripto feliciter emenso*, Romae vel alibi cursum theologiae ampliorem perficiant." There is some difficulty in carrying out this decree, as far as Rome is concerned, as we believe that the English College is not meant for those

wish on behalf of those of average ability that, if
there is to be a central college, the studies may not
be too advanced, and that the solid instruction of all
be not sacrificed to the brilliancy of a few.

There are many other points on which we should
like to touch, such as the alleged difficulty of getting
competent professors, emulation, relative expense,
on which we cannot quite agree with the writer of
the article; but we have said enough to show that
there is a very distinct other side to this many-
sided question.

We venture, then, with all deference and respect to
the exalted authorities with whom the responsibility
of decision rests, to submit the following considerations: (1) That while for small dioceses the best
and only method is to unite temporarily in a joint
Seminary, it would be retrogression and not progress
for larger dioceses, which can stand alone, to make
a new departure of that kind. (2) That perhaps the
time has come for carrying out, where it is possible,
what the Council of Trent decreed, and our own
Councils have desired—namely, the separation of
clerical students from laics, even in the early years of
their ecclesiastical training, to the great advantage of
the former. (3) That our Seminaries should provide

who have already finished their course in England. Students are
generally sent there for seven, six, or four years. Many people
question the advantage of this practice. If older students could be
sent to Rome, it is said that they would derive greater profit, as their
minds would be more mature, their health would not be so likely to
suffer, and a larger number would be able to have the opportunity
of residence in Rome, as their stay would be of shorter duration. In
this way the want of a college of Higher Studies in England would be
to some extent supplied.

a course of study suitable for an average student.
Hereafter we may look for a college of Higher Studies
if the foundations are well laid in the Seminaries.
In such a college the more gifted from the various
dioceses would come together with minds matured
and prepared. Then, indeed, would be the eager
contact of mind with mind, and the life and vigour
which are born, not of mere numbers, but of talent
and culture, and which are not fully attainable in
any Seminary where men of all different capacities are
united, and where the few talented ones soon make
themselves known, and retain their pre-eminence
throughout.

II.   An Alternative Policy and Its Feasibility.

Tablet, March 18th, 1893.

Through the kindness of the editor, to whom we
offer our sincere thanks, we were enabled last week
to offer some remarks on the establishment of a
proposed central college for the South of England.
We propose now to state what seems a preferable
plan. We trust that we shall not seem wanting in
respect to our ecclesiastical superiors, with whom
the decision rests. We feel sure that, when a
momentous reversal of policy is being suggested
and perhaps urged, they will be glad to have information from any source, and to know the thoughts
passing in men's minds. Our only reason for writing
is the single desire that the best course may be

adopted, and the fact that we have had some oppor-
tunities of getting information on these subjects, and
of forming an opinion on them.

1. It would be easy to show that where a Diocesan
Seminary is possible, it is a source of strength to the
diocese. It is a centre for the clergy, a bond of
union, and it will encourage and increase the development of vocations. This is true, though for
accidental reasons in some places these good results
have been neutralised. We need not, however,
dwell on this, but we prefer to take our stand on
the admission made by the writer of the article of
March 4th, namely, "The separate Diocesan Seminary represents the Church's ideal for the methods
of ecclesiastical education." What we plead for,
then, is that that ideal should be ever before our
minds, that we should do nothing to hinder or retard
its realisation ; that, in a word, there should be some
kind of continuity of policy, without which there will
be no real progress. We plead for this in oppo-
sition to a policy which would be retrograde, which
is justified only by explaining away the decrees of
Councils, and which could not possibly be final and
permanent for even one diocese. The policy so
repeatedly urged by the late Cardinal Archbishop is
undoubtedly true and according to the mind of the
Church : this statement is not vitiated by the fact
that the said policy has been carried out in some
cases prematurely, or without sufficient concentration
of resources, and, therefore, without success. This
want of success is, moreover, no reason why we

should adopt a policy which might, perhaps, have been serviceable thirty years ago. Father Morris, S.J., sketched clearly and commended the late Cardinal's policy in his article in the *Month* of February, 1892.

As matters stand now, it would appear that three dioceses at least in the South are in a position to have Diocesan Seminaries for the education of their students in Humanities, Philosophy, and Divinity. Westminster has had a college ever since its erection into a diocese, and it seems hardly credible that the Ordinary, Chapter, and clergy would be now willing to forego their privilege, especially as they have the glory of possessing the oldest college in England. May we be allowed, in passing, to offer to St. Edmund's, the *Alma Mater* of so many hundreds of priests, the tribute of our sincere filial gratitude and love. Birmingham seems well provided in this respect. Southwark thinks that it can stand alone, and is gradually forming a true Seminary, *ad mentem Concilii Tridentini.* Why, then, should not these three dioceses be content with attaining the Church's ideal?

But what, someone may ask, is to become of the smaller dioceses? Is not a central college needed for them? We venture to think not. Those dioceses which possess Seminaries have, probably, accommodation not only for present, but for future needs, and there must be, for a time at least, vacant places in their Seminaries. Why should not these places be occupied by students from the smaller dioceses?

2

There need be no question of conflicts of jurisdiction
or of joint administration, which would remain with
the Ordinary of the Seminary. There are sure to
be differences of system and education in the different
Seminaries. In one it will be deemed that preparation for the London University ensures sound
education, while another will consider that a true
liberal education is better attained by some other
method. In one diocese no lay students will be
admitted, in another it will be considered prudent to
continue the united system. One Bishop will give
shorter and another longer periods of vacation.
There is no need for absolute uniformity, and needs
and circumstances vary even in different parts of the
same country.

Might not the Ordinary of each of the smaller
dioceses, then, choose that one among existing
Seminaries in which he finds the rules and education
most in harmony with his own views, and arrange
to place his ecclesiastical students there? Later on,
if he has reasons to be dissatisfied, still more if, as
we must all hope, his diocese develops, as years go
on, to such an extent as to be able to act up to the
Church's ideal and to have its own Seminary,
he will be able to withdraw his students without
any heart-burning, and without inflicting any real
loss on the diocese which has given hospitality
to his young levites during the time that their
own diocese could not afford to do so. This,
we submit, would be a constructive and not a de-
structive policy, leading gradually, prudently, and

surely to the realisation of what the Church wishes
—a separate Diocesan Seminary in every diocese
which is capable of having one.   Surely if we have
any belief in the probability of even a partial conversion of England, we must admit that every
diocese will be in this position some day or other.
A central college, especially under joint jurisdiction
or administration, would retard and hamper the
realisation of this ideal.

2. Now as to the question of the studies to be
pursued in the Senior (Philosophy and Divinity)
Section of a Diocesan Seminary.   We submit, for
the reasons given last week, that they should be
solid but not too elaborate, meant for the average
student ; also that, as a general rule, all students
should go through the ordinary course.   We have
in view such a course of study as is followed in
many Seminaries abroad.   It consists of one or two
years of Philosophy (Mental Philosophy and
Natural Science), and three years, often nearly
four years, of Divinity (Dogmatic and Moral
Theology, Church History, Canon Law, Liturgy,
Ascetics, and Pastoral Theology).   The Scripture
lectures are often extended over the years of both
Philosophy and Theology.   Such a course has been
found by practical experience to ensure a *scientia
competens* to the average student, while it affords at
the same time a solid grounding and plenty of scope
for extended study to the more gifted.   If Natural
Science is sufficiently studied in Humanities, there
is not quite the same need of two years of Philos-

ophy, though it is considered very advantageous. Again, all students should go through this course, save in rare cases. It is not fair to the Seminary to withdraw the best men from it and send them elsewhere ; this practice may lead the other students to regard their studies with some contempt, as though fit only for mediocrities. The Seminary course should be elementary, but solid and serious, with nothing to be despised in it. Another reason is, that with our very varied work in England it is much to be desired that all should be well grounded in every subject. Now it has been stated on good authority that students sometimes return from a long course abroad, even with a Doctor's cap, and with a great store of dogmatic learning, but knowing little of Morals and less of Ascetics or Pastoral Theology. This is a misfortune, and such a Doctor is not so well fitted for parochial work as his less gifted colleague who has had a sound Seminary training.

It is evidently desirable that there should be, if possible, some external incentive to earnest study in the Seminaries, and some means of creating a wholesome, but not exaggerated, emulation among them. Would it not be possible to arrange for an examination to be held every year, not for the South only, but for the whole of England, for the degrees of Bachelor of Divinity and Bachelor of Canon Law.* The *Institut Catholique* of Paris

* Of course, we mean such degrees as those given at Louvain or in Paris : the Roman B.D. would be of little use, as it would not ensure a satisfactory standard at the end of the Seminary course.

does this, and the examination, the programmes of
which are before our eyes, is so arranged as to
enable a student of fair ability to obtain one or both
of these degrees at the end of his Seminary course,
if he has worked properly during it.   The pos-
sibility of obtaining this degree would be an incentive to earnest work, and the examination would be
a common aim for all the colleges.   Their Lord-
ships the Bishops could surely obtain from the
Holy See authority to confer such degrees, and
could arrange such an examination.   In addition to
its being an incentive to ordinary students, it would
be an advantage to the more gifted, who are to
proceed elsewhere for Higher Studies after their
Seminary course is completed.   They would then
have only the Licence and the Doctorate to proceed to.

3. This brings us to the question of Higher
Studies, which, we submit, should succeed, not
supplant, and be distinct from the Seminary course.
Our ideal would be that, when most of the dioceses
are properly equipped with Seminaries there should
be a central college of Higher Studies, like those
at Louvain, Paris, Lille, Fribourg, and other places,
to which the more gifted students might proceed
for a longer and higher course, after their spiritual
formation had been completed, and the Priesthood,
or at least the diaconate, received.   But we fear we
are not ripe for this yet, though it may be surely
looked for hereafter as the crowning point of the
edifice of ecclesiastical education in the country, *if*

only we do not stray from the right path now. But meanwhile, why not make use of existing Universities abroad, which would afford our best students the highest teaching, the practical knowledge of some foreign language, the breadth of mind which is so opposed to our native insularity, and an idea of the state of the Catholic Church in other countries. This method would sufficiently supply our wants, till our own resources are more developed and there would be nothing retrogressive in it.

4. It has been said that expense is against the formation of separate Seminaries. We have good reasons to doubt this. If a diocese is sufficiently developed to have its own Seminary—and we believe that this is the case when it needs and can support seventy to one hundred students—we feel sure that the expense per head will not be so great as the pension at present charged in many colleges. But to obtain this, all the students of the diocese, Divines, Philosophers, and Humanists, must be concentrated in *one* Seminary or college, not scattered in several.

5. A last point for consideration is the question of forming a teaching staff, a very important matter, but not of the huge difficulty which is often asserted. Foresight must be used and care taken to pick men in advance, and to get them special training for their work, if it is necessary, either at home or abroad. This is done elsewhere and might be done in England. Of course, there will be periods of difficulty and weakness, but these are found in every good

work. We need solidly instructed, painstaking, devoted masters, and not extraordinarily brilliant men, who as a rule cannot, or at least do not, teach well. Alas, we know too well the would-be brilliant professor, who can never be satisfied with any text-book, however renowned the author, but must be ever making emendations and additions, wearing out his unfortunate students with endless dictation, which is crammed for an examination, and never looked at again. From such eminent professors may our Seminaries be preserved!

In view of these considerations, we ask what real gain there would be to the greater dioceses of the South in departing from the ideal of the Church and uniting in a central college. In all humility, we venture to think that it is of vastly greater import-ance to Westminster to have a true Seminary within its jurisdiction, than to have a school of commer-cial instruction, if the two things are incompatible. It has been announced that the centenary of Old Hall as an ecclesiastical college is to be kept this year. Edmundians may well ask, with sadness, if they are to celebrate at the same time the fact of its being, perhaps, somewhat less an Ecclesiastical Semi-nary now than it has ever been before.* Is there anyone, who has been made acquainted with the facts of the case, who will maintain that it would be right for Southwark to abandon the work after which it has been striving for twenty years, which was

---

* We rejoice to learn from the President of St. Edmund's that the number of Church students is not only maintained, but is increasing.

repeatedly urged upon it by the highest ecclesiastical authority in the country, for which so many
generous benefactors have denied themselves, which
is already gaining a fair measure of success, and
which aims at realising the ideal of the Church?
From the form which the suggested change of policy
would take, it is possible that Birmingham might
profit thereby; but it would scarcely desire to do so
with the consciousness that other dioceses would at
the same time be injured. If this change is adopted,
those responsible for it will, it would seem, be very
unlike the late Cardinal Archbishop, who, as Father
Morris tells us, in this very matter, "showed his
usual wisdom in preferring, with a smaller present
benefit" (if, indeed, it be smaller), "a plan more
permanent in its character, where the outlay of the
present is an investment for the future" (*v.* "The
Cardinal Archbishop," by Father Morris, S.J.,
Month, February, 1892, p. 167).

We have spoken out the thoughts which were in
our mind, as we conceive that the suggested new
departure would be a grave mistake. If we have
said a word which our superiors may regard as dis-
respectful or presumptuous, we desire to withdraw
it, and we assure them that it is not so meant. But
the matter regards us all, clergy and laity alike, and
we feel justified now in opposing a suggestion which,
should it ever become a decision of authority, it
might, perhaps, be unseemly even to criticise. This
decision rests, ultimately, with our chief pastors; and,
in concluding, we desire to assure them of our abso-

lute respect, submission, and obedience in this and
every other matter.

III. OUR RESOURCES AND OUR MODELS.

In the *Tablet* of March 25th a leading article appeared referring rather than replying to the points
which we urged in the previous articles. After
reading this leader very carefully, we feel that
we can stand by all that we have said, and that
no adequate attempt has been made to meet the
points that we urged. We are not responsible,
moreover, for some of the ideas imputed to us in the
reply of the *Tablet*. We advocate separate Diocesan
Seminaries, where they are *possible;* not quite the
same thing as the *present system* of Diocesan
Seminaries. We nowhere advocated "a work of
undoing and subdivision." We wish to use present
materials in building up, we have no wish to destroy:
this belongs rather to the other side. We neither
expressed nor implied the slightest wish "for the
suppression or radical transformation of all our
existing diocesan colleges" or "the speedy establishment" of substitutes for them. We do not
look forward to any such thing. We merely suggested that perhaps the time has come for the
separation of clerics from laics in places where it is
possible, fully recognising, as our words show, that
in very many cases it would be either imprudent
or impossible to do so. As the whole question of
the ecclesiastical education was being raised, it

seemed right to declare our conviction, founded on a somewhat exceptional experience of the two methods, that the separate system is by far the best. We believe that this will be of more importance in the future than many are conscious. Some time ago, we are told, the separate education of clerical students was described as a hothouse system unsuited for English boys, or words of similar import. Our experience does not allow us to admit the fairness or the accuracy of this characterisation : let those testify who know. But, on behalf of the advocates of separate education, it seemed opportune to recall to those by whom it is disregarded or disliked, that this system is most certainly the method decreed by the Council of Trent, and desired by the Provincial Synods of Westminster. The members of the latter probably knew English boys well, and were also fully aware of the "Catholic character and spirit" of our colleges, and of the other conditions of their existence, and yet they made the decrees which we have cited. The words which we have quoted are to be found in the *Tablet*, and there are other remarks as to "half-a-dozen centres," "handfuls of diocesan Divines," "a staff of professors to be recruited from each Diocesan Seminary," and others which do not touch anything that we have advanced, but seem rather to obscure the issue. It is necessary to say this much to define our position in the two previous articles, though we do not understand how the misapprehension arose.

There were, however, two or three points in the

article of March 25th which it is necessary to treat at greater length.

1. First, as to our resources. We are as fully aware, as the advocates of a central Seminary can be, of the needs and requirements of a modern Seminary, and, moreover, we know as a fact that they are fully met by such a course as that which we described last week. We called it *elementary* as opposed to the higher or University course : it is a distinctly fuller course than that which has been usually adopted in England up to the present time : it is in no way elementary as being incomplete, or as aiming at a low standard. We say this, as some have misunderstood the term. Such a course does produce excellent parish priests, and, moreover, assures to the more gifted students a sound basis in *all* branches of ecclesiastical learning. The latter, when they have finished it, pass to higher courses of special study elsewhere, and many attain great eminence. We could cite many instances among our personal acquaintance, and among those who were our fellow-students, to prove this. Some are engaged in parochial work, and are admirably fitted for it ; while others, all of them quite young men, are attaining great distinction in those special branches of study which they have taken up in Universities or elsewhere since they completed their Seminary course and received ordination. At the same time, whether they are more or less gifted, they possess without exception a *scientia competens* for *all* their priestly work.

We believe that more than one diocese in the South of England could provide such a course as we have in mind, and that it would be amply sufficient. Of course, it cannot be brought to perfection in one year or two, but will become more and more complete every year, if a *continuous* policy is carefully followed out. With continual change, nothing of lasting worth is possible anywhere.

A direct question was asked in the *Tablet* as to the Chair of Scripture, which is admittedly a difficult one to fill. But it is quite possible to find competent men to undertake what is necessary in this respect, if we go the right way to find them. Only compassion can be felt for the young students, who, at the outset of their Scripture course, are entrusted to the first-rate Biblical scholar, engrossed in the higher criticism. Such an one will not enter into their needs or difficulties, or inspire them with confidence, unless he be a man of rare humility and self-effacement. In the Scripture course the greatest care and judgment must be used to make it really practical and not to extend it in the wrong direction. It seems a great mistake to concentrate all the attention of the students on one or two books of Holy Scripture, and to allow them to pass out of the Seminary with a very poor and inadequate knowledge of the Bible as a whole, of inspiration, and such like matters. This is sometimes done. However, the writer did not explain his idea of a suitable course of Scripture for average students, so that it is unnecessary to dwell upon the matter. We may, perhaps, be advancing views in harmony with and not opposed to his own. But throughout his article he seems to us to exaggerate our difficulties and minimise our resources in every respect.

2. Again, we are *very much surprised* to hear " that the model of a Theological Seminary, as far as studies are concerned, is the *Collegium Romanum.*" We have some knowledge of the history of Seminaries, and we are satisfied that this statement is quite inaccurate, and that it is shown to be so again and again by the action of the Holy See. The *Collegium Romanum* most certainly has *not* been the model of all other Seminaries ; we find no proof that it was ever meant to be such, and it does not necessarily represent " the mental training which the Church has invariably demanded for three hundred years and more." There are strong reasons why it should not be taken as the best model for England. Persons of information and experience have told us repeatedly that it is not wise to send students to Rome, unless they are of more than average ability, as the course of study is not adapted for them, and that they will not derive profit from it. It is certain, also, that, when ordinary average students have been sent to Rome, they have sometimes returned home literally " overburdened with a mass of undigested matter." They have been thus less fit for their work than if they had had a simpler course in England. The full curriculum in Rome has been generally and rightly regarded as a higher course for the more gifted, though it does not attain the

level of some other Universities. It is not the model for an English Diocesan Seminary to follow.

Surely, in a matter of this kind, where experience is almost everything and theory is of little value, it is very narrow to look merely in one direction, even though it be to the local usages of Rome, usages which the Holy See has not followed in legislating for other places. We suspect that the writer of the article in the *Tablet* has little practical knowledge of studies in France and Belgium, of what is understood by a Seminary course there, or of the results attained thereby. There is an immense deal to be learnt from both countries. This whole question of Seminary and University studies was very fully discussed some years ago in France, and settled in the sense which we have advocated. We would strongly advise those interested in the matter to read M. Icard's *Traditions de la Compagnie de S. Sulpice pour la direction des Grands Séminaires* (Paris, Lecoffre). In the third part, in the chapter entitled " Enseignement des Grands Séminaires. En quoi il diffère de celui des Facultés Universitaires," he enters fully into the question, and shows why the French Bishops decided to maintain the usual course of study in the Seminaries, and to require all students to pass through them, and to provide a higher course in the Universities for those who wished to *specialise* later on. M. Icard's experience and authority are, perhaps, unique ; and all may learn from him, even where they do not fully agree with his views.

The writer in the *Tablet* has referred to Belgium
and to the Faculty of Theology at Malines, which
was afterwards transferred to Louvain. We have
already shown in our first article that the Belgian
practice and the rules in force at Louvain are entirely in favour of the course which we are advocating.

Italy, on the other hand, is a very unsuitable
country to take as a model, as the study of Philosophy and Theology there comes after a system of
secondary education, very unlike ours in England.
It is very misleading to speak to us of a three years'
course of Philosophy which is really occupied with
a good deal of work, which at home is done in
Poetry and Rhetoric, or even lower down, as well as
with Mental Philosophy. Our meaning will be clear
if reference is made to the charter just given to Milan
(September, 1892), where it is laid down that after
the *ginnasio* are to come three years of *disciplinae
philosophicae* comprising also the other studies of the
liceo, namely *Latin, Greek,** *Italian, Civil History,*

* We do not suppose that those who proposed the *Collegio Romano*
as our model would wish us to take its standard for Greek or
Mathematics.

It may interest some to know more of the charter given to Milan,
which restores the old Faculty of Theology to the Archiepiscopal
Seminary of that city, not that it may absorb other Seminaries, but to
give the Province the means of granting degrees. There is a clear
reason nowadays why in Italy the faculty must be attached to a
Seminary, and not to a University in the natural fashion. Under the
present Government the existence of a full Catholic University is, we
believe, an impossibility. Even in France the Catholic Universities
are *legally* only "Instituts." By this charter, after the course of Philosophy described above, there follows an *ordinary* course of four years
of Theology, consisting of Dogma, Moral, Scripture, Canon Law,
Church History, Sacred Eloquence, a few lectures on Thomistic
Philosophy, and an optional course of Hebrew and Greek. There is
a *special* course of St. Thomas, but only for those preparing for the
Doctorate, for whom a fifth year of study is required. Only those who
have passed the "Licence" are admitted to it. Students of the

Natural Science, Mathematics, as well as Christian
Apologetics, Logic, Metaphysics, and Ethics.   This
is very different from what most English readers
would understand by a three years' course of Philosophy.   We affirm, without fear of contradiction
from those conversant with the matter, that the
course of studies now attainable in France and
Belgium is considerably higher than that found in
Italy, in some respects even than in Rome itself,
and that the degrees are of distinctly higher value.
This is, probably, why the Bishops of the United
States—so we are informed on good authority—
have taken so much account of these countries in
arranging their system of education, and especially
in the establishment of the Washington University.
The circumstances and methods of these two
countries are more akin to our own than those of
Rome.   In Rome, as far as can be learned, an attempt
has been made to unite and mingle an ordinary and a
higher course of studies.   The result of this has been
to produce a course rather beyond the average student,
at least as a preparation for such work as exists
in England, though it is less unsuitable for many

Province who proceed to the Milan Seminary, after having completed
the ordinary course in their Diocesan Seminary, in order to become
Doctors, have the special privilege of proceeding Bachelors and
Licentiates in one year, and Doctors as soon as one year is complete.
The ordinary course of study is very much the same as we find in
France and Belgium, the degrees are much easier, *e.g.*, Louvain
requires eight or nine years of Theology before the Doctorate, Paris
at least seven ; Milan is satisfied with five ; Rome with only four.
There is clear evidence in this charter that the *Collegium Romanum*
is not taken as the model.   The charter is dated September 20, 1892,
and is therefore a very recent piece of legislation.   The course of
study prescribed in it is that of a quasi-University ; the standard for
a Diocesan Seminary is admittedly lower.

Italians who will not take faculties or enter on parochial work till much later on in life. On the other
hand, it has undoubtedly led to the gradual lessening
in meaning and value of theological degrees, so that
nowadays a Roman B.D. carries hardly any value,
the S.T.L. is not worth very much more, while
the Doctorate has no longer the worth and dignity
which belonged to it in times gone by, or which
still accompany it in other places, at Louvain for
example. At the present time the Louvain B.D.
represents almost as much study as the Roman
D.D., while the licence is of distinctly greater
value, entailing as it does a theological course of
from six to seven years. Of late the Roman degrees have acquired somewhat increased importance, but it is hardly accurate to maintain that
the Roman colleges have maintained the highest
standard in the past, or have served as models to
the rest of the world.*

Reference was made in the *Tablet* to Perugia and
the efforts of the present Holy Father, when he was
Bishop of that see. We are not in possession of
all the facts of the case, but we know enough to

* At Louvain, two years' study of Theology, *in addition to* the three
or four already completed in a Diocesan Seminary, are usually required
for the B.D.; and two more for the licence. After becoming a
Licentiate, the student passes two years in private study before
proceeding to the Doctorate. A public defension is required for
all degrees, even the B.D.
In Paris no student can present himself for the B.D. "nisi in
doecesanis seminariis integrum tum philosophiae, tum theologiae
curriculum per quadriennium saltem cum laude fuerit emensus."
The interval before the higher degrees is the same as at Louvain.
In both places those who wish to become Doctors must have com-
posed a treatise on some subject. These are often two hundred pages
in length, and must be of real value.

show that they do not tell against our contention. Neither have we any fear of an adverse decision of the Holy See, if *all* the facts and circumstances of the case are fairly submitted, as the decisions already given in similar cases are not unknown.

3. The writer made some remarks about the distinction between Greater and Lesser Seminaries. The division seems to be in the main a matter to be determined by circumstances and convenience. In large dioceses it is a necessity on account of numbers; *e.g.*, in Paris there must be between six and seven hundred clerical students, and these could hardly be united in one building : as a matter of fact, they fill no less than four distinct establishments. What does seem of importance is that the Senior Section of a Seminary (Divines and Philosophers) should be rigorously separated from the Junior Section or Humanists ; and this is perfectly practicable, even under one roof, if the building is properly arranged and suitable rules are made. They need not come across each other save in the refectory, where they have different tables, and in the chapel. But they hold no communication with one another, and practically form two Communities under their distinct superiors, though all are under one Rector or President. The separation is important : the Divines are young men, the Humanists are mostly boys ; and, though the principles of training are the same, and should be continuous, yet the application of them will vary in many accidental ways. Subjects of spiritual reading

and meditation,* the order of the day, and certain
rules cannot and ought not to be same. There are,
however, distinct advantages to be gained in having
the Divines in the same house, though not in contact with the juniors. Their presence lends dignity
to the whole establishment, they are a perpetual
reminder to the juniors of the future before them,
the services of the Church are better carried out,
and the ordinations are certainly a lesson and an
encouragement to even the youngest students, when
they witness them. The union, then, of the two
sections in one house is quite feasible ; it has distinct
advantages, while possible disadvantages may be
neutralised by foresight. Financially, the gain is
very great ; and such a method, with our smaller
numbers in England, appears almost the only
prudent one. It is clear that some dioceses can
maintain a Seminary of their own, there is hardly
one which can keep up two or three institutions of
the kind at the same time, and the attempt has
already resulted in disaster. By keeping all our
students in one place, we have only one staff of
servants, one set of farming expenses, one burden
of rates, taxes and tithes, etc., to provide for. As
the students grow in number, the cost per head
continually decreases, and all the resources of the

---

* Provision for having these exercises apart may be made by having
either different Conference Rooms (*Salles des Exercises*) or separate
small chapels for them. The whole Community can unite in the
principal chapel for Community Mass, visits to the Blessed Sac-
rament, Benediction, and the solemn offices of the Church.

diocese can be concentrated on the one establishment.*

The position of the whole question has somewhat altered since the first article appeared in the *Tablet*. It is now publicly known how Southwark will act, and that it will be true to the ideal of the Church. No one can rejoice more than we do at the growth and success of Oscott. *Floreat in aeternum.* That the Birmingham Seminary should be a help and a centre for weaker dioceses is precisely what we advocate and desire. We trust that it may attain the highest available standard of culture and excellence, and be, perhaps, a light and a guide to younger institutions. But we still oppose from a Catholic, no less than a diocesan, point of view, the suggestion that all dioceses should be called upon to take part in a common college, whether they feel the need of it or not. This was, undoubtedly, being urged. We need emulation among institutions no less than among the individuals in each Seminary. We can never hope to have a

---

° A suggestion was made that our junior students might be kept in the Seminary here, and then sent for their Divinity to the proposed central college. Apart from the fact that such a course would be contrary to the Provincial Synods and to the object for which the Seminary was built, a very little reflection will show its utter impracticability. The Seminary is built on a scale to hold all our students, it is necessarily expensive to maintain, and the resources of the diocese would be quite inadequate to maintain it in a half empty condition, and at the same time to pay away a large sum to another Seminary for the education of the Divines. Moreover, it would be more expensive to keep thirty students in the central college than the same number here, so that it would be necessary to materially lessen the number of our students, or it would become impossible to maintain equilibrium between the two places. We may add that those who have made generous sacrifices for the establishment of a really complete Seminary for Southwark might justly complain if the work were now abandoned, or mutilated in an essential respect.

Louvain or a Washington University in England unless we first have Seminaries in sufficient number to feed it with the best men trained within them. It is of the very essence of a true college of Higher Studies, still more of a University, that it should receive students from many various quarters. Without this it will have little life. It is not a question of mere numbers. There will be more vigour and mental work among twenty picked men than among sixty average ones with only a few brilliant ones in their midst. We need a college of Higher Studies, and, no doubt, in due course it will come into existence. But we repeat what we said in our first article. The Seminary and such a college are distinct things in aim, in methods, and in discipline, and no permanent good can be produced by trying to graft one upon the other. The result would be to produce a course of study beyond the capacity of a large number of students, but not equal to that which is expected in a true college of Higher Studies. This is not a state of things that anyone would desire, who is concerned for the future development of theological study in England.

IV. On the Separate Education of Ecclesiastical Students.

In the foregoing articles we have incidentally expressed our strong conviction that it is best that Church students should be educated apart from laics during the whole period of their ecclesiastical training : in other words, that only those who show some marks of vocation, and have a real desire to become priests, should be admitted to our Seminaries.* We are not aware that this question has been treated publicly before, and, as it is one of very great importance, it seems opportune to enter more fully into the matter. At the outset we wish to express the earnest hope that we shall not be regarded as criticising the system pursued in our old established and venerable ecclesiastical colleges. Nothing is further from our mind. Educated in great part ourselves at Ushaw and St. Edmund's, both as lay and clerical student, and owing to those noble colleges a debt of gratitude greater than words can express, it would ill beseem us to be the critic of our *Almae Matres*. We are glad to have this opportunity of expressing to those colleges and to those who were our superiors there, our deep and lasting gratitude and affection. We wish to consider the question on its own merits, and more in reference to what is advisable in the future. But the very fact that we owe our own training to the older colleges, that we have there seen the mixed system at its very best, and that our whole inclination would be to cling to the traditions that we know so well, will, perhaps, add some weight to what we have to say as to the superior advantages of training our Church students by themselves. It will be advisable, for the sake of clearness, to ex-

* May we be allowed to refer our readers to an article in *Pastoralia* for June, 1893, where we have stated what we consider may fairly be expected from those who wish to enter a Seminary, either at their own expense or on a diocesan scholarship.

amine first the reasons usually adduced in favour of the mixed system, and then to state the reasons on the other side.

I. 1. The strongest argument is that the system of union has hitherto prevailed in England, that it has proved successful, that it has formed most excellent priests, and, in short, is one of our traditions. No one can be more averse than we are to breaking with a long established custom, especially if we find that it is based on principle. When, however, the history of this system is examined, we find that it arose from two urgent causes of *expediency*, not from any conviction that it was the better course ; and that it was adopted and has been maintained with some hesitation and reluctance. The two causes were, first, the scarcity of Catholic schools to which boys of the higher classes could be sent ; and, secondly, the impossibility of maintaining the colleges by means of the Church students alone. The united system was adopted, therefore, on account of a peremptory necessity, and in advocating separation we feel that we are following on the lines which would have been adopted by the founders and early rulers of our old colleges if they had lived under changed circumstances, and had been able to carry out into action the principles which animated them.*

There can be no doubt that this system has been

* Strong confirmation of what is stated here may be found in various places in the very able and most interesting *History of St. Edmund's College*, which has just appeared from the pen of the Very Rev. Bernard Ward. See also *Conc. Prov. Westm. III.* (Decr. XIV.).

wonderfully successful, and has produced priests of the highest excellence. This is no matter of astonishment. God has blessed the efforts made for the education of the clergy under circumstances of great difficulty and necessity. Now that difficulties are less and the necessity no longer the same, it may well be asked whether the union will produce the same results. All we maintain is that by separation greater results may be maintained in the direction to be pointed out later on.

2. A second argument often used is that the separate education has prevailed in France, and that, in consequence, there is now a great gulf between the clergy and laity there. It is astonishing how persistently this statement is made, and yet *it is devoid of all foundation in fact*. Want of sympathy no doubt exists to a far too great extent in certain parts of France, between the priests and their flocks, but the alleged cause does not exist. As a matter of fact, for the same reasons as in England, namely, the want of good Catholic colleges after the Revolution, and the difficulty of maintaining purely ecclesiastical colleges, the so-called *Petits Séminaires* in France are, with very rare exceptions, really mixed colleges like ours in England. It is not until Philosophy and Divinity that the separation takes place, and even then the students are away from the Seminary and living at home for nearly *three months* of the year. During the last twenty years, especially since Père de Foresta began his Apostolic schools, there has been a notable increase in the number of

Petits Séminaires of an exclusively ecclesiastical character. This change has been made for the reasons which we shall state later, and has been productive of great good. But it is a distinctly new departure, and the enormous majority of the clergy of France have been educated in a closer contact with the laity during their Humanities than our own in England.*

3. A third reason given for the union is that thereby a good understanding is promoted between clergy and laity in after life, and that lasting friendships are formed. We doubt this latter statement very much, unless the intercourse is closely maintained after the lay students have left and the clerics are engaged in Divinity, and this is not often the case. The lasting friendships of life are not made between fourteen and eighteen, unless they are maintained by intercourse during the early years of manhood. With regard to the former statement, it

---

° This is not the place to write an essay on the Church in France, but many real reasons of a far different nature might be given to explain the separation alluded to.

There are some people who seem to think that when they have said that anything is French, Italian, German, etc., the question is settled and that such a thing is necessarily bad. It is difficult to argue with such, but surely their position is illogical. There are, no doubt, many practices in every country so bound up with and dependent upon characteristics, which are exclusively national, that it would be unwise to introduce them in another country. But there are many others also which owe their origin to a really *Catholic* tradition, and these it is not well to reject contemptuously. On the other hand, there are many things in England which are the outgrowth of Protestantism, and which were unknown before the Reformation, and it would be foolish to cling to these merely because they may now be called English. It is wiser to judge and adopt practices in each case on their own merits without too narrow an adherence to national prejudices. Of course, where any system is truly consonant with English character, untainted by Protestantism, there is a strong reason for following it in dealing with English boys or men.

seems clear that there is an equally good understanding, at least in the South of England, between
the clergy and the laity educated at purely lay
schools as with those who have studied in the mixed
colleges, and that a priest will find sincere friends
and helpers among the former quite as much as
among the latter. Practical experience is the only
test of this argument. Moreover, however much
this mutual understanding may have been promoted
in the past, when colleges were few, it is hardly
worth while considering it now, seeing that the
great bulk of our laity are already being educated
in purely lay schools, and this tendency for various
reasons is largely on the increase.

4. A fourth reason is drawn from the good effects
produced on the lay students, that through the union
some receive vocations. This is true, but in order
that the argument should have weight, it would be
necessary to show that the vocation would have been
withheld by God if the students had studied elsewhere, and we must set off against it the vocations
which have undoubtedly been lost among clerics
through their contact with the laics. We are writing in the interest of ecclesiastical students, and we
are not concerned with lay education ; but we may
say, in passing, that it is better for laics to be
educated in a really good lay school than in a mixed
college in many cases. It is said that this was one
of the motives which lead to the foundation of the
Oratory School. When a college attempts to prepare for divergent careers, it cannot attain the

highest success in any, as the methods of training are different in so many respects.

It has sometimes been said that lay boys, often having had a better early home training, do good to the clerics in supplying the deficiencies of the latter. We do not believe this, and the question is not one to discuss. Should there be any such deficiency on the part of the young Church students—and it is not improbable, seeing that the Holy Ghost does not restrict vocations to one class of society—it can be easily, effectually, and perfectly remedied by superiors themselves, if they will only live on intimate terms with their students, as we shall say hereafter, and pay a little attention to these matters. Of this there is no doubt.

II. We have tried to state and meet the usual arguments advanced in favour of the union of clerical and lay students. We proceed now to give our reasons for advocating entire separation. All that will be said applies exclusively to the students in Humanities, i.e., from Figures or Rudiments to the end of Rhetoric. It is already conceded that Divines should be alone, and, as we have said in the previous article, we contemplate a Seminary where the Humanists form a community quite distinct from Divines and Philosophers, either in a separate house, or in a different part of the same building. Our remarks refer to the junior section, or Humanists, only. We say, then, that it is better for our students to be entirely alone during their Humanities, for three reasons. First, because it is

the wish of the Church. Secondly, because thereby
much greater attention can be paid to the formation
of character and to spiritual development. Thirdly,
because fewer will abandon their vocations, and
those who have no vocation will discover the fact
much sooner.

1. Few words are needed as to the wish of the
Church in the matter. Enough has been said in
the first article. The meaning of the Council of
Trent is clear, and the Synods of Westminster show
that its decrees are applicable and ought to be carried
out, wherever possible, in England. There is no
real dispute on this point.

2. We maintain that a better training can be
given ; and this is really the point on which the
whole matter turns. What is the meaning of Seminary life : what did the Council of Trent intend?
Most certainly, the solid spiritual formation of the
future priests. There were schools in existence
three hundred years ago ; there are many such now,
under pious and prudent teachers, to which our
students could be sent, if it were merely a question
of obtaining good teaching for them, or if the clergy
were expected to be just the same in character
and training as pious laymen, and nothing more.
But this has never been the mind of the
Church. A secular priest requires an education
sui generis, which will fit him for his special work.
His position is one apart, of quite exceptional
difficulty and responsibility, and demands a most
special preparation, a more careful one than that of

a religious, for more depends upon it. A religious has round him his brethren and his superiors, he has a constant rule of life to check or stimulate him. A secular priest, on the other hand, at twenty-four or twenty-five, is placed in the world, practically alone, with no one upon whom to lean, and all men depending upon him, and that, perhaps, for a long life, and throughout he has only the training of his Seminary career to sustain and help him on his course. His education, then, is not that of a religious, though the foundations of supernatural virtue must be quite as deeply laid : neither is it the training that is given to one who is to pass his life as a layman in the world. It is a special formation which will fit him at an early age to pass out into the world with a character strong and manly enough to stand by himself, to bear the wear and strain of life, to be in the midst of the world and yet not of it, and to continue faithful and steadfast in the great responsibilities which he has of his own free will, in response to the call of God, taken upon himself. Such a future certainly demands real and solid supernatural virtue; and all will admit this. Moreover, it claims, secondarily, perhaps, but almost as much, a due formation of natural character. A priest needs not virtue only, but the highest possible development of what is naturally good in human character. It is not too much to say that in every walk in life greater positive harm is frequently done by some crookedness or twist of natural disposition than by actual wrong-doing. Everyone knows of instances

where truly holy men are rendered almost useless
by some defect of character which might easily have
been corrected in earlier life. This, then, is the
second great work of Seminary life; to train and
develop character in those who are to be the
ministers of the Church to all kinds and conditions
of men in every class of society.

Now it is manifest that such a training in virtue
and of character is no easy task, and requires considerable time. It is not wise to leave it until the
last three or four years, and to let the student pass
the most impressionable years of life, from fourteen
to twenty, when his character is really changing,
without the constant thought of the career that is
before him. During those years he is no longer a
child, but his character is still pliable, and has no
fixed habits ; he is capable at that time of the most
generous efforts, and his mind is accessible to the
highest ideals. There is no other such time in the
whole of his life, and if it is allowed to pass in a
heedless way, the work that could have been done
then will never be possible in the same degree
again. At twenty he will have drifted into an un-
formed but fixed disposition which will strengthen,
as he grows older, but which will rarely change.
We are lead, therefore, to the irresistible conclusion
that the chief and greatest part in the formation of
our future priests must take place *while they are in
Humanities*, and that those early years are of vastly
greater importance in their ultimate consequences

than the later years which immediately precede ordination.*

Lastly, that training and education will be the best which are most fully based on the motives which are to guide a priest through life, so that there may be no abrupt transition from his life as a Humanist to his life as a Divine, and then on to his life as a priest in the world. As far as possible it should be one continuous evolution, varying no more than age and accidental circumstances render necessary. What are the leading motives which are the safeguard of a priest, and will maintain him in all the strength and fervour of his vocation. None other than his vocation itself, his dignity, his Priesthood. These alone, but they are enough, if once properly conceived. These, then, should be the motives and the mainspring of his life *throughout* his preparation, if they are to hold the same place afterwards, when he is ordained and launched alone upon the world to face his responsibility.

If these things be granted, namely, the necessity of special training, that it should be going on during the years of early youth, and that it should be based on such motives—and they are not likely to be denied—we say that the Ecclesiastical Seminary,

* We are told that Cardinal Wiseman used to say, in reference to another matter, " give me the boy from fourteen to nineteen and you may do what you like with him afterwards." This is quite as true with regard to clerical students.

The present Cardinal, in the preface to the *Life of St. John Baptist de Rossi*, says : "The priest is not a layman in Orders, on a social level with the attorney and the doctor. Everywhere he stands alone, associated with the Apostles for the conversion and salvation of the world ; and he needs *their* spirit " (p. lii.) Is it not in early youth that he must imbibe it ?

properly constituted, is able to do a work which a mixed college is hardly able to attempt, however excellent it may be. Let us trace the path of a clerical student in either case.

He goes to a mixed college, his only motive being that he believes himself called to the Priesthood, and desires to prepare himself for that end. When he arrives, he finds himself in the atmosphere of a truly good Catholic school, with the same aims and ideals placed before him as before Catholic lads who are to live as laymen all their lives. Higher motives, his vocation, and the thought of the Priesthood, are sometimes alluded to in Confession, in Retreats, etc., but they are not *prominently* before him as the motives of his life. He finds that the ordinary school-boy view of rules and obligations is generally received and tacitly accepted by authority. He sees that rules may be and are evaded, and the consequences cheerfully taken. A variety of such consequences are provided for different cases, such as lines, limits, tasks, extra study, or more painful ones, in order to ensure discipline and promote study. Later on, competitive examinations may be proposed to him to attain the same end.†

† It is not necessary to enter into the question of studies here. It is sometimes said that an external examination is required to make students work. We should be sorry to think this of Church students, and it would be very sad. The examinations pass, and what is to take their place as an incentive afterwards in Divinity or in the Priesthood; and what is to be the incentive for those who know that they are sure to fail, owing to incapacity for certain subjects. The real use of an outside examination seems to be to keep us in touch with the general education of the country, and this is of some importance. As an incentive it ought not to be allowed to have more than a very secondary place. There are higher motives which will lead earnest students to study quite as efficaciously. Are those who will work only for external

He finds that he is under the control of a prefect of discipline, and of masters of various degree, not merely as teachers, but to maintain the observance of rules. These rules are regarded as matters of slight consequence, and it is considered rather as the province of a master to enforce them than of a student to keep them. In many cases our student will have little intercourse with the priests in the house, save in class and in Confession, and will regard them and speak of them more as professors and masters than in their priestly character. We do not allude to these things by way of criticism, but merely to show that during these years he will be receiving little more than the training which is needed for a lay student, and based upon the same motives. What is the result of this? In the case of a really earnest student, little loss will be sustained; his own generosity and thoughtfulness will make up for defects of training, though he will hardly attain his full perfection of character. An average student, fairly earnest, who has gone to college with a real idea of doing his best to prepare for what he knows to be a high vocation,

success really the men that we need? How did people do before these examinations were introduced?

There are some who conclude that if a college does not prepare for such examinations, education in it must be at a low ebb. This is unfair and unreasonable. There are some who feel conscientiously that they are promoting solid education more effectually by abstaining from such examinations, especially from those of London University. The question is an open one, and liberty may be fairly claimed. If any external examination is adopted it should be a suitable one, which will aid and promote true education. There are certain examinations which would seem to have a decidedly opposite effect. Are those who are of this conviction to be blamed for not adopting them, seeing that their sole reason for such a course is their concern for education, and not their neglect of it?

will be disappointed and astonished at first, but will soon be acclimatised and settle down to his surroundings. Such an one. presently, tacitly acknowledges to himself that his previous ideal was an exaggerated one, that it is not necessary to aim so very high, when one is going to be *only* a secular priest, and that any striving after perfection is not required, as such a thing is rarely or never alluded to. But it is on those who are naturally heedless that the absence of special training tells most fatally. They pass through their college life, good perhaps, but with no adequate sense of what they are preparing for, and thinking of little more than of leading good Catholic school-boy lives. Some go on this way to the end, even to ordination—the testimony here is not our own, but that of those of far greater weight and experience—and the burden of the Priesthood is accepted not unworthily, but all too heedlessly, because their student life has been heedless through want of training. Others, when they come to the last years, realise at length what they are about, fear the state which they have so far never seriously contemplated or prepared themselves for ; they pass out of the college, and are stranded, often for life. A vocation which was true has been lost for want of careful culture. These things are admitted very generally, and it is no fault of our colleges that these results are brought about. It is quite impossible to give an adequate training to the clerics without at the same time placing before the lay students a standard which for them would be unreal and exaggerated. But it is quite possible for a clerical student to pass through the whole of his Humanities without receiving any *special training* beyond that of his lay companion, and with his character hardly affected; those most precious years are lost in this respect, and will never come again.

Moreover, there are positive dangers from the contact of lay students. That of worldliness was pointed out by the Councils of Westminster, and is greater as time goes on. Lay boys often come from very worldly homes, and many instances could be given in which their influence has been very harmful to the clerics, making them extravagant in their ideas as to expense, and dress, and amusement. Good students are thus often led into the error that because they are all alike in colleges, they may take just the same standard as their lay companions in all these matters. It explains also why clerical students in vacation time sometimes indulge in a manner of life and dress in which all thought of their vocation seems laid aside, though all the while they are at heart very excellent fellows. Other dangers might be alluded to, were it necessary to dwell upon them. But it is manifest that where the union exists, it is almost impossible to train the clerics to the practice of the sacerdotal virtues of simplicity, detachment, interior obedience, and the rest, of which the Synods speak, and, as a matter of fact, little attempt is made to do so.*

* It is not rare to find students who, after several years passed in a mixed college, leave it with an absolutely incomplete idea of what their vocation demands of them. When they realise it they sometimes ask

Now, let us follow a student into an Ecclesiastical
Seminary, where he will find none but those who
have the same aspirations as himself, and where he
will have opportunity to realise all he may have set
before himself in wishing to prepare for the Priesthood. He will find a rule drawn up with only two
objects in view, the one to preserve the necessary
order of the community, the other, to help him in his
own training. He will be told, at the outset, clearly,
distinctly, and repeatedly, that he should remember
what he has come to the Seminary for ; that he
is aiming at a high object, and that he must be in
earnest about it ; that superiors can only show him
the way, and that his progress in virtue and learning
really depend upon himself ; that he has come to the
Seminary of his own free will, and that he is quite as
free to leave if he finds, after experience, that the
life does not suit him ; that he must be generous
and resolute in overcoming himself and correcting
his faults if he desires to obtain his end. It will
be pointed out also that, while the rules of the
Seminary in no way bind under pain of sin, they
cannot be neglected without fault in many cases or

not unnaturally, " Why were we not told these things before ? Nothing
was said to us at college about the Priesthood or our vocation, or that
we ought to be so much in earnest about it. It would have been better
and easier for us if we had understood it sooner." The position of
such students is less favourable than that of one who has studied in a
purely lay school and then enters a Seminary in Philosophy. The
latter comes to the Seminary knowing that he is entering on an entirely
new career, and prepared to act earnestly and up to a high ideal. The
former have for several years been under the false impression that they
were preparing themselves for the Priesthood, while, owing to their
easy-going life, they were doing nothing of the kind. It is much more
difficult for them to rouse themselves afterwards and adopt a higher
standard if they see the need of doing so.

without real harm to himself, as they really constitute
the duties of his state of life, and are laid upon him
by legitimate authority ; and that, if he finds them
too irksome, it would be better to take to some other
career, because he will have much greater difficulties
and responsibilities to meet with as a priest.* He
will be told also that, while he need not fear punish-
ment for breaking these rules, he is expected to
observe them loyally of his own accord ; and that
from this superiors will naturally judge how far he
is in earnest, while at the same time they will make
all allowance for age and forgetfulness. These things
will be explained in Retreat, in frequent spiritual
conferences, and in the more intimate relations of
superiors with individual students. What is the
result of such a system ? The boy finds that he is
met on the very ground which has brought him to
the Seminary, namely, desire for the Priesthood ;
he is treated rationally, his sympathies are enlisted
on the side of rule and order, because he feels that
he is accepting them of his own free choice in view
of his end, and he understands that they will do
him little good unless he makes them his own, and

* Compare the words of St. Charles (*Institutiones Seminarii*, Pars.
III., cap. 1) :—" Adolescentes, qui singulari Dei beneficio sunt delecti,
ut in Seminario instituantur, id potissimum intelligere debent, cujus
gratia Concilii Tridentini Decreto Seminaria instituta sint ; et intelli-
gentes, saepius animo repétere, omnesque nervos intendère, ut illud
divina ope suffragante, ad animarum salutem, ad Ecclesiae utilitatem,
et Pastorum solatium consequantur.
" Quod si qui propter improbitatem, aut negligentiam, illud minus
obtinebunt, aut quia sua ipsi sponte ab instituto Clericalis vitae rece-
dant, aut suo vitio a Seminario expellantur, vel Episcopo suo parere
nolint, in iis rebus quae ad ejus Ecclesiae utilitatem spectant, cujus
sumptibus aluntur et educantur; *graviter peccabunt* atque a Deo,
tamquam alienae facultatis usurpatores, accerrime punientur."

endeavours loyally to act up to them.† The thought of the Priesthood, his vocation, and his conscience guide and direct him and his companions ; and the whole organisation of prefects of discipline, penances, dormitory masters, study-place masters may be abandoned without fear of disorder or difficulty. The students can be fully trusted to manage their own affairs ; and any check or restraint required for the younger ones or for new-comers is quietly and gently supplied by their older companions, without it being necessary for the latter to be in any sense masters, or ceasing to be their fellow-students. The action of superiors becomes almost entirely directive and little more. This is no fancy picture. We have seen it elsewhere ; it has fallen to our lot to work upon these lines here, and no one who has not had experience of it can realise what effects will be produced. If students are fairly treated in this way, we can affirm that absolute trust may be reposed in them. Rules will be well kept, they will study hard, and the work of superiors will be easy. Meanwhile, all that is in the nature of boys to do, they will do and do well; their games and amusements will be fully entered into, and all that is bright and good in their time of

---

† Compare *Prov. Conc. West. IV.*, Decr. IV. 18 :—" Moreover, it must ever be apparent that rules from without in reference to progress in virtue are of little avail, unless they are willingly and cheerfully accepted and kept by the student so that they serve not to the eye but please God from pure hearts. Beautiful is that maxim of St. Charles, laid down in the institution of his Seminary, to wit : ' The acquirement of virtue depends mainly upon the earnestness and industry of each one, rather than upon the care of rectors and masters, so that the endeavours of others will avail little or nothing, unless one sets to work himself.' "

life will flourish. But underlying all a solid, earnest, manly piety will grow up, without anything sentimental or passing in it ; and prayer and study will have their due place too, and they will succeed well in all their intellectual work according to their ability. Trained in such a way, accustomed to keep a rule of their own accord, to study by themselves, not under a master's eye, the same life will go on when their position changes and they become Divines ; it is not likely to alter when they are ordained. Accustomed to act from boyhood up under the law of liberty, for conscience-sake, of their own free will, they will have acquired the virtues which a secular priest needs beyond all others.

Moreover, their character will be well formed, first by their own efforts, secondly by contact with their superiors and companions. They of themselves keep rules without external pressure ; this cannot be done without constant self-renunciation and generous self-conquest, which react powerfully upon character. The nature, necessity, and means of acquiring different virtues are often put before them. Either in public or privately their attention is directed to their faults of character, and they are able to overcome them. The importance of so doing is not allowed to pass unnoticed. The friction of daily intercourse with companions, all with the same aim before them but of varied disposition, helps also to the same end ; but the most potent influence is undoubtedly the free, familiar, and intimate terms

on which they are able to live with the priests who
are their superiors. In mixed colleges, as a rule,
there is a great separation between professors and
students; the latter, in many instances, rarely see
the former save in class, and regard them with a
certain timidity and act towards them with reserve.
The head of the college, above all, usually lives in
a region apart, and is not often approached by junior
students, and then only with some trepidation. We
do not now enter into the reasons of this practice;
but in a Seminary it is quite inadmissible, and it is
disastrous in the case of clerical students anywhere.
There is a saying in Ecclesiasticus which aptly
represents what the position of Superiors should be :
" Have they made thee a ruler ? Be not lifted up :
be among them as *one of them*, have care of them "
(xxxii 1 and 2). The same thought is expressed by
the Fourth Council of Westminster : " It is greatly
to be desired that, as Christ lived in the midst of
His Apostles, so also should the rector of the Seminary, together with those to whom the teaching of
the students is entrusted, live *in common* with the
Seminarists, and both by word and example instruct
correct, and console them " (Dec. IX. 7). After all
this is the way in which all good work has been done,
by pagan philosophers of old, by our Divine Master
Himself, and by those who have trodden in his
footsteps : no power on earth can take the place of
direct personal influence. The effects are gradual,
often imperceptible, but deep and lasting, and
whereon will a more loyal affectionate respect be

given to superiors than where such mutual relations exist. Such intercourse is very necessary. The students are sent to us to be prepared for the Priesthood ; they have a claim on our patience and consideration beyond all others ; in a few years they will be our brethren in the ministry. How better can they acquire the spirit of their state than from the priests who live in their midst, not as masters or prefects to maintain discipline, but as elder members of the one same family, taking and evincing interest in all that concerns the members of it. Moreover, there are numberless things which interest or worry a boy during his course, which are in no sense matters of confession, and which will only do harm if he has no outlet for them. The Church takes him away from his home, from those who are his natural advisers, and this for most wise reasons ; but it is our duty to make up for their absence and let him feel that he is living with those who are only too glad to listen and to be of service to him. Otherwise he will keep such things locked up in his heart, for boys are very shy in some respects ; or speak of them only to companions, who from want of experience cannot advise him well. All who know college life will admit the truth of this, and numberless vocations have been lost in this way. A further result of this daily common life is that insensibly deficiencies of early education are corrected, and all kinds of topics of conversation are opened out for the students, so that a real and wide education is continually going on quite apart from the mere work done in school ; false impressions are corrected, true judgments suggested, and wider horizons unfolded before the students without any effort, merely from contact with older minds. If boys are left for their society entirely to themselves, there is no chance of their rising much beyond their own level ; and they will have purely boyish un-developed thoughts about all kinds of things not merely till the end of Humanities, but, unfortunately, for a long time after, in many cases.

It is thus, then, that in a Seminary a real work of formation in virtue and of development of character is perpetually going on, guided and directed by superiors, but *really the work of the students them-selves*. We have stated nothing that is not abso-lutely true, and we think the picture a more satisfactory one than the life of a student in a college where lay students are admitted. In the latter case the motive which has brought the cleric to the college, and which is to rule him in after life, namely, his vocation to the Priesthood, is in the background, while ordinary school-boy ideals are prominently before him, good in themselves, but far less than he is capable of, and essentially transient as he gets older. In the Seminary, on the other hand, his vocation is *throughout* the motive of his student life, as it will be that of his priestly life here-after : the one will be but the continuation of the other without break or interruption. This is surely what is to be desired. What is the result of such a training ? That the most earnest and gifted students will receive their most perfect development; average students will steadily improve and approach more and more closely the ideal set before them; the naturally heedless will, from the beginning, be forced to look their future in the face, and will not waste precious years in a desultory half-hearted manner; they will have to make a clear choice between doing their best as clerical students, and embracing some other career. All will give hope of being at the end of such a course men of formed character, and of real virtue, and of promise for their future labours.

We are conscious that some will say that such a training is an ideal one, quite impossible of realisation, and beyond what may fairly be expected of boys. We can only answer: try, and your opinion will soon change. We are assured by those who have far greater experience than our own, that it is quite possible, nay, easy to carry it out. We have seen it elsewhere, and have known its great results. For four years it has been our duty to undertake it ourselves, and it has succeeded beyond our hope or anticipation. Our slight experience fully justifies the wiser heads who advocated this course, and promised that it would succeed if fairly tried. We are convinced that no boys are more ready to adopt high principles, and to aim at a lofty ideal of honour and conscience, that none are more capable of being trusted than are our English Church students, if only the opportunity be given them. Again, we say, let those who doubt them in this respect try the experiment fairly and they will not have reason to repent.*

* Intimately connected with formation of character is the question of vacations. Formerly it was the custom to keep Church students at college almost the whole of their course and to allow them to go home very rarely. Latterly this has been modified, and it is the more general custom to permit them to pass the vacation with their friends. This new procedure seems far wiser. To our mind the vacation is an integral and essential part of a student's training, and should *always* be passed away from the Seminary. Should it be impossible for a student to go home, owing to loss of parents or other reasons, he should be sent elsewhere, but he ought not to remain in the Seminary. The change is important for his health, it is still more vitally so as the test of his vocation. He is called to live in the world, and it is good that he should keep up the holy and sacred home relations as far as possible. Moreover, the vacation should be in miniature what his whole life is to be hereafter. He understands that, while there is rest from study and he is more his own master, there is *no* vacation from spiritual duties, and that he must learn betimes to be a rule to himself and stand on his own legs. His conduct during the vacation is the touchstone of the value of his training during the year. If daily Mass, spiritual reading, prayers, and other spiritual duties are neglected then, he knows that he must fortify himself and strengthen his character on returning to the Seminary. If in the following years he finds no improvement, he may well ask himself whether he would not be safer in a Religious Congregation under a constant rule. If, on the other hand, as will usually be the case, he finds that in the main he is faithful, and more so as he gets older, and that spiritual duties, etc., do not suffer through absence from the Seminary, he may have reasonable confidence that he will be man enough and strong enough to be faithful and generous when he leaves the Seminary for the last time and enters on his priestly life in the world. We need not point out to directors of conscience the incalculable value of this part of a student's career, which is passed out of the Seminary, as a test of the reality and strength of a supposed vocation.

On the other hand, the recent practice of long vacations adopted in many places seems more open to question. Christmas vacations especially appear best spent in the Seminary. Many great feasts of the year come at that time, which it is well for students to celebrate together : the change at that season is of little use for health : there is danger, too, for *younger* students of their forming a quite false idea of life in the world, from their being thrust at that time of the year by imprudent friends into all kinds of excitement and amusement, so that they feel no longer the same relish for the college life, and take a long time to settle down again. For summer vacation, a clear month or at most six weeks seems sufficient. This is sufficiently long for health, to keep up home relations, and as a test of stability. Nothing is gained by prolonging the time. Most of our students spend their vacation in the same place, often in town, and they have no great variety in it such as boys of the highest classes have. Moreover, a long vacation is an unnecessarily heavy expense for many parents. Acting, too, on the principle that the Seminary life should be a distinct preparation for the student's future life, it seems reasonable to limit

3. Our third reason for advocating separate education, is that fewer will abandon their vocations, and those who have no vocation will discover the fact much sooner. It is admitted that the number of those who enter our colleges as ecclesiastical students, and who leave without receiving the Priesthood, is very great. Some leave through health or family reasons, and this will be the case everywhere : others retire through want or loss of vocation. The number is variously estimated : in some dioceses it is placed at fifty per cent., in others a lower rate is given, in others again even a higher percentage is admitted. It is not rare for students, after five, six, even ten or more years in college, to abandon their contemplated career. This is a great pity, the loss of men and means is very great. The

their absence to about the same period as will form their annual vacation after ordination. Still more by requiring them to pass Christmas away from home, and by restricting their period of absence in the summer, we bring home to them, and to their parents, the fact that, as they have received a different vocation, so they must be prepared to be treated differently in these respects from boys of their own age who have not the same high calling. No greater service can be done to a student than to bring before his mind, as early and forcibly as possible, that in seeking the Priesthood he is aiming at a life which is essentially one of self-sacrifice, and to give him some opportunity of showing his willingness to practise it. If a clerical student grumbles and is discontented because he is allowed home only once a year, and then for a shorter time than students in a lay college, he shows that he does not realise adequately the favour which God does to anyone in calling him to the Priesthood, that he has little gratitude for it, and is not yet capable of the life of self-renunciation which he professes to desire. Our predecessors in the Priesthood one hundred years ago had to make much greater sacrifices of home and comfort to attain their end. The students of to-day ought not to be so degenerate, or their parents either, as to shrink from the much smaller sacrifices which are now asked of them. The Fourth Synod says : "Since the seminarists are called to leave the *conveniences* and *comforts* of worldly life, and to devote themselves wholly to God and the salvation of souls, they should shun contact with the world and not even at vacation time visit their relations without the Bishop's leave."

result on the individuals who so leave is often disastrous. They enter on life with an education and habits unsuited for business, at an age when other young men have already gained some experience and position. There is hardly any condition more difficult than theirs. We venture to think that with an education such as has been sketched, the number of those who *give up* would be very materially reduced, and that they would do so much sooner. Experience has shown that in a purely Ecclesiastical Seminary a large number may leave during the first year, if the candidates have not been carefully selected, but that *very* few will do so in the higher classes. If the candidates have been well chosen in the beginning, hardly any will leave even at the outset. To obtain this result, it is well not to admit students until they have ceased to be children, and can form something like an intelligent conception of what they really aim at. St. Charles put the age at fifteen. In England, at present, fourteen appears the lowest age, except in rare cases: often, if a boy's character is still that of a child, it is safer to wait a little longer. Students should not be received unless they can realise that they are going not *merely to school*, but to prepare for the Priesthood. Then it is found advantageous to give them a time, as it were, of probation during the first months of their stay in the Seminary, during which they can find out whether they like the life which they have to lead, and superiors are enabled to judge whether the aspirants are disposed to be in earnest or not.

They are not allowed to regard themselves or to be considered as really belonging to the Seminary until this time is passed, and they have asked spontaneously to remain. If the decree of the Council of Trent is carried out, and the students wear the cassock, they are not allowed to wear it until this period of probation is over, and superiors are able to give a favourable account of them to the Bishop. This time of trial can easily be prolonged if there is reason for doubt in the matter. If such a practice is adopted, it is certain that very few indeed will leave later on. As we have said, the students are made clearly to understand from the outset what their life is to be, what the preparation for the Priesthood requires, and what is expected of them. Having chosen this freely themselves with their eyes open, they are happy in it and are not very likely to swerve from it afterwards. If, when six months or a year have gone by, a student does not appear to see his way clearly or shows little earnestness, it is judged best to advise his return to his friends. If later on his path is clearer, and he wishes to make another attempt, he will, perhaps, return ; and such students often turn out well, as they act with greater deliberation. But it is thought wiser not to allow any to remain unless they show an earnest spirit and give promise for the future. It will be little loss to a student to spend a year or two in a lay college, or in the world, and then return thoroughly in earnest, and be ordained a few years later in consequence of the delay. But it might do him irreparable harm to remain on in the Seminary in a half-hearted style till eighteen and nineteen and then *give up*, only to find his prospects of success in the world seriously compromised on account of his age. Students are able to leave the Seminary with little hesitation or difficulty; everyone knows that it is only those who have real vocations who can remain, and no kind of disgrace attaches to those who leave. They remain on good terms with the authorities of the Seminary, and there is no heart-burning on either side. For all these reasons the loss of students is small, and nearly always occurs only at the beginning of the course. Naturally, in this matter, the experience of others engaged in the same work is far greater than our own, as being of longer duration; but our own slighter knowledge fully confirms their testimony.

We have now expressed our conviction that it is best to educate our clerics alone, and stated the chief reasons on which that conviction rests. We have seen the two methods at work, and no shadow of doubt remains in our mind as to which is the better. All, we believe, who have had the same experience, will agree with us. Many, no doubt, will not admit our conclusions at first. We only ask that they may be fairly considered, and not condemned at once. One thing we can assert, that we have not exaggerated, and that we have drawn no fancy picture; we have but set down what we have known and seen, and we are not without hope that our statements may be of interest, and perhaps of use, to those who have at heart the great and most important work of the due formation and training of the future Priesthood of England.

In concluding these articles it is well to say that no claim to originality of thought or matter is made for them. All that has been said will be found in various places, and has been gathered from many sources and from the experience of many competent persons. In some cases reference has been given to certain books, most often it is impossible to state whence the idea comes; the thought is remembered, but the place or person whence it came, perhaps several years ago, can hardly be recalled. Much will be found in the Synods of Westminster which are full of the most useful matter on these subjects. Amongst English books, it would be a want of gratitude not to say that none has contributed more to form our convictions regarding the mental culture and spiritual training of our clerics than the very able essay of the present illustrious Archbishop of Westminster, which is prefixed to the *Life of St. John Baptist de Rossi*, a work which we have read again and again, always with fresh profit. It may be gratifying to His Eminence to know that many of the suggestions there made as to the value of the study of English, the study of portions of the Fathers concurrently with the classics, the use of sodalities, and the standard of life to be aimed at, and other points, have been kept steadily in view, and are being carried out in the Southwark Seminary.

We ask those who read this little book not to pay attention to the writer, but to give a fair consideration to the matter which it has been his duty to bring together.

Spes messis in semine.

www.ingramcontent.com/pod-product-compliance
Lightning Source LLC
Chambersburg PA
CBHW022020080426
42733CB00007B/664